Kevin Durant

THE STAR

DAVE JACKSON

Intro

Kevin Durant is one of the most highly touted and talented young basketball players currently active in the National Basketball Association, where he plays for the Oklahoma City Thunder as a small forward. His high-profile career, whilst still in its infancy, began as a college player, in which he only need to play one season before being called up to the big leagues.

From his debut season in 2007, aged just 19, Durant has gone on to gain some of the best awards in the entire NBA, including Most

Valuable Player and being a four time scoring champion. Still only 26, Kevin Durant has quite the career in front of him, and his rise to prominence should be an inspiration to any young aspiring basketball players.

Early Life

Kevin Durant was born on September 29th 1988, in Suitland, Maryland not far from Washington DC. His parents divorced from a young age, which saw his grandmother playing a strong parental role alone with his mother. One of four siblings, he has a sister named Brianna and two brothers named Anthony and Rayvonne.

Naturally tall from a very young age, Durant was often the subject of ridicule from his classmates, and cites his grandmother's insistence that his height was a gift as a one of the key influences that led him to playing basketball, which he did from a young age.

Durant would play Amateur Athletic Union basketball from a young age, playing for various teams throughout Maryland. He began his career in this league at the PG Jaguars, a team based in the Prince George's County of Maryland. Success came early for Durant; as he would go on to win two championships with the Jaguars during his time there.

A mentor and coach to Durant named Charles Craig had an early influence on the young star in the making. He was tragically murdered at the young age of 35. To this day Durant pays tribute to his lost friend and mentor, wearing the number 35 in honour of the age in which Craig died at.

High School

Despite being over 6ft when starting high school and already established as a very promising young player, Durant would continue to grow, reaching an imposing 6'"9 in his time at high school. In these years he would play for several different teams. These included the National Christian Academy and Montrose Christian School – both of which were located in Maryland. He would also Oak Hill Academy, one of the more reputable high school teams that played in Virginia.

In his final season as a high school player, Kevin Durant's skills and technique were gaining a fair amount of attention from the press. He was quickly touted as one of the best talents to emerge from 2006, and soon featured in a number of top lists for various publications.

USA Today and Parade Magazine named him in their first team All-American lists, and he shared the MVP honours in the MacDonald's All-American Games, which saw him gain 25 points for the West squad. The season also saw him lead Montrose Christian to an impressive 20-2 season.

This would garner the attention of many college teams, all of who wanting to gain Durant's signature. The offers even came in from Division I teams, showcasing the true potential that Durant had.

The University of Texas Lognhorns would eventually be Durant's team of choice. They had spent much time courting a young Durant in high school, having sent out assistant Russell Springman, who was from Durant's native Maryland, in his freshman year. These extra efforts had swayed one of the most highly touted young basketball players in the country, and his first season of college basketball would prove to be more than fruitful.

College Career

Kevin Durant's importance to the Longhorns was clear from the beginning. Even in his freshmen year, he would start every game for the team. It would prove to be a wise decision, as Durant would only serve to one term in the college basketball leagues.

That season was more than successful for the young Durant, where he would go on to average 25.8 points per game – the highest in his own conference the Big 12, and fourth overall in the entire country. Not only that but he would average in 11 rebounds per game in a total of 35 league games for the season.

He would also go on to score more than 20 points in 30 games, and exceed 30 points in 11. The season earned him a selection of top awards. After being named the Big 12's player of the year and freshman of the year, he was also the first ever college freshmen to win the Adolph Rupp Trophy, the Naismith Award and the Wooden Award.

He also received several other player of the year awards which saw him named in the First Team All-American Honours, being only the 3rd college freshmen to do so. Add this to several scoring records that were set in the Big 12 conference, and Kevin Durant's one and only college season turned out to be one of the most prolific ever, which is rather impressive considering he was only a freshman!

NBA

After a more than successful debut season in college, Durant took the bold step to declare himself eligible for the 2007 NBA Draft. Even as only a freshmen, Durant had garnered many would-be suitors, and was eventually the second overall pick in the draft. The team that won the rights to sign him was the Seattle Super Sonics, making one of two first pick drafts who were only freshmen – proving just how much potential the rookie had.

His debut for the Sonic's would come on October 31st, where he would make an immediate impact on the game. With 18 points, 5 rebounds and 3 steals, it was a performance worth remembering, and would set the high standard that Durant would play to for the entire season.

It would not take long after his debut to score a match winner, as a game against the Atlanta Hawks on November 16 gave Durant his first taste of glory. He would go on to be a pivotal p[layer in the Super Sonics season that year, as they struggle to maintain regular form, yet Durant would remain one of the bright sparks in this period.

Overall, Durant's debut season was more than impressive. Considering he was still only 19, yet still the number 2 draft pick for the year, he took the responsibility well and showed the extent in which his abilities would grow. Gaining the Rookie of the Year Award, Durant wound up with an impressive season average of 20.3 points, 4.4 rebounds, 2.4 assists and 1 steal per game.

This would put him in esteemed company, as he has since been one of only 3 players that include LeBron James and Carmelo Anthony to score an average of 20 points per game whilst being only teenagers. Add the fact he had previously negotiated a Nike sponsorship of upwards of $60million, placing him only behind LeBron in earnings from a Nike contract, and the sky was the limit for Durant.

There would be a sudden change in surroundings for Durant, as the Seattle Super Sonics decided that they would be relocating to Oklahoma City to play as the Oklahoma City Thunder. The start of the 2008 season saw Thunder draft Russell Westbrook, who would go on to develop a very strong partnership with Durant.

The season would be another improving year for the developing talent. He would start 74 games in total, and would increase his average stats from the previous season. With an increases average of 5 points, his impressive 25.3 points per game would get him ranked 6th overall for scoring in the entire NBA. His overall stats increased, with averages of 6.5 rebounds, 2.8 assists and 1.3 steals all improvements from his debut season.

Particular highlights for this season included a then career high points total for a game with 47 against New Orleans. The newly minted franchise Oklahoma City Thunder needed records to be set and Durant duly obliged, with 24 free throws one of his notable achievements. He also gained the highest point tally ever in the Rookies Challenge at the start of the season, netting 46 points. This would see him nominated for the Most Improved Player Award, which he came third in.

The 2009-10 season would prove to be a breakout seasons for Durant, who would go on to establish his status as one of the best forwards in the NBA. As this was only Thunder's second season as a franchise, expectations were low for the team, which was notable for the amount of young promising payers in their ranks, with Kevin Durant at the forefront of this.

With upset victories over some of the biggest teams of the NBA such as Orlando Magic and the LA Lakers, as well as other notable big hitters like Miami Heat, Boston Celtics and the San Antonio Spurs. Durant was one of the main reasons for such unexpected success, as he would continue to flourish in his star role, again increasing his stats for the season.

He played every single game of the 82 game season, and became the youngest player to win the scoring title with a monstrous average of 30.1 points per game. Added with his incredible records such as 756 free throws, back to back 40 points games as well as a franchise scoring record of 2,472 Durant had earned his first ever spot in the All Star team, and finished second in the MVP voting.

This form saw Thunder finished with a very respectable record of 50-32, more than double their debut season, showing just how far the team and Durant had come in one year. With an unexpected play-off spot secured. Despite losing to defending champions the LA Lakers, Oklahoma City Thunder made more than a good showing of themselves, with Durant scoring 24 points on his debut playoff game against the Lakers.

Kevin Durant was at the front of this young and ambitious team, who were now being touted to make quite a bit of noise in the next season. They had a young and vibrant squad led by one of the NBAs biggest starts in Kevin Durant, along with strong home crow attendances and financial stability, Thunder were now one of the hottest teams in the NBA.

Prior to the start of the 2010-11 season, Thunder fans were given some great news, as Durant had signed a five year contract extension with his team. The deal was worth approximately $86 million, and was a perfect example how far Durant had come in his few short seasons in the NBA, now being the top player for his team, and one of the best overall forwards in the league.

Durant would be the leading scorer in the NBA for a second year running (only the 11th player to do so), averaging with 27.7 points per game. Thunder had also improved their results from the previous year, winning 55 games in total. These impressive efforts would earn him a spot in NBA First Team for a second time after the previous season.

A shortened season in 2011-12 would see Durant take his team all the way to the playoff finals, in which they lost to Miami Heat. Durant would lead the charge in this challenge, averaging with 30.6s per game. His overall season average was 28 points per game, gaining him the scoring title for a third consecutive year, representing the fact he was now one of the best forwards in the entire NBA.

He also managed his first 50 point game, with 51 scored against the Denver Nuggets. Scoring 36 points in the 2012 All Star Game, he would win his first ever All Star Game MVP award. His status as one of the new stars of basketball was becoming more obvious, as scored 30 plus points in the first four games of the season, with

Kobe Bryant being the last player to achieve this back in the 2005-06 season.

2012-13 was not as successful for Durant, as he would not finish with the scoring title for the first time in 3 years. He made up for this by increasing his shooting rate percentage to 51, his three point rate to 41.6% and a free throw shooting rate of 90.5%. This would put him in the illustrious 50-40-90 club, firmly cementing his status as one of the best all round shooters in the NBA.

The following year would end up to be Kevin Durant's best season yet. Averaging with 32 points per game, as well as scoring 30 plus points in 12 straight games, which included a career best of 54 points scored in a single game, Durant was near unstoppable. Finishing with average rebounds of 7.4 and 5.5 assists per game, he was finally awarded the elusive Most Valuable Player Award. Despite this, Thunder still could not find playoff success, losing to the San Antonio Spurs in the conference finals.

Unfortunately for Durant, the following season would prove to be one riddled with injury. Suffering a fracture at the start of the season, he went on to miss the first 17 games, returning in December. After suffering a few more injuries in December and January, Durant decided to get some surgery done to help with injuries. In March, he was officially ruled out for the remainder of the season, meaning he only managed to play a career low of 27 games – yet with an average of 25.4 points, 6.6 rebounds, and 4.1 assist per game, he still managed to impose his skill set.

Impact in Basketball

Kevin Durant's first 8 seasons in the NBA have been some for the most successful for a young player. Debuting after one year as a college freshman, he has shown the value that can be placed on the young developing players found in the college leagues. He stated his debut season as a raw talent, and with the proper development has developed into one of the best forwards in the entire world of basketball.

With Oklahoma City Thunder, Durant has had a team built around his skills, with a strong importance placed on youth. With this set up, he has had some of the best seasons that a young player ever has; win is shown by his records. With 6 All Star Team places, 4 scoring championships (3 back to back) and an MVP award, Durant has blossomed into a young star.

As a small forward, he is traditionally smaller than other players in this position standing at 6'9. He was even criticised for being too slim, and not too much of a well-rounded player. Despite not being the fastest or strongest, he has managed to improve all aspects of his game, such as his passing and defence. Having improved these stats every year from 2010, he showcases how far a young player can go with hard work and proper development.

He is also one of the most well liked players in the entire NBA. As a charitable and friendly person, Durant has donated millions to various charities, and is held in high regard throughout the country. This nice guy image is a rare one for a sportsman, yet Durant has proven how it can be done and to great success – his jersey is a regular best seller amongst all NBA players.

Future

Aged only 26, Kevin Durant has a more than bright future ahead of him. Even with is recent injury setbacks, he is still one of the highest valued players in the league, and one of the best scorers to grace the NBA. He only as one season left on his current contract, which will see him become a free agent in 2016.

While many teams may try and lure Durant away from Oklahoma City Thunder, he has stated on several occasion how much he enjoys playing there. Yet rumours will always be around, and with talk of him wanting a return to Washington DC, there is always the chance Durant will try his luck elsewhere. One thing for sure is that on his current form, he will have his pick of teams looking to sign him; it is all down to what Durant wants for himself.

Conclusion

Kevin Durant has showcased just what it takes for young player to succeed in sports. Working hard and being dedicated from a young age will bring you closer to realising your dreams of being a professional sports player. Reaming humble throughout, Durant has showcased a hunger to improve and learn even after he is established as a top player, and these are the characteristics that could see him potentially becoming of the greatest basketball players of all time.

Anyone who dreams of playing not only basketball, but any type of sports, should look towards players such as Kevin Durant. Whilst he has obvious natural talent, he has not just relied on that, he has taken the time to better himself and players around him. He also shows loyalty to those who have helped him reached where he is today, and is the perfect role model for any aspiring sportsperson.

From the Author

Thank you very much for downloading and reading this book. I hope that you find the information useful and interesting.

If you enjoyed the book, please take a moment to share your opinion with other on the book page.

Still craving for more interesting basketball books? I recommend you to check out my other books below that are also available for a great price.

KOBE BRYANT
The Legend

DAVE JACKSON

LEBRON JAMES
The Greatest

DAVE JACKSON

Photo Credits

Keith Allison

Erik Drost

aaronisnotcool

Copyright

Made in the USA
San Bernardino, CA
12 January 2017